# VIVAT SAINT PETERSBURG

# Vivat SAINT

Anatoli Medvednikov

# PETERSBURG

*Art-Park Publishers*

*Saint Petersburg, 1993*

Photographs and text by Anatoli Medwednikow

Designer Alexander Lobanow

Translated by Catherine Phillips

The author would like to thank the sponsors
of this book:
Hotel Saint Petersburg, The Astoria Hotel,
Hotel Pulkovskaya, Tourist Company
St Petersburg-Intourist,
Pan-Tour Tourist Company

CONTENTS:

# The Birth of St Petersburg

*When* you arrive in St Petersburg you will enter on one of the most amazing pages in the history of your life. As you step across the threshold of the great city, you find yourself simultaneously in several centuries of history of the Russian State.

The chronicle of St Petersburg, written in stone by many generations, can be read like an open book on the squares, streets and avenues of the city, boldly set out on the page by the hand of Peter the Great centuries ago.

On 27 May 1703, Peter I laid the first stone of the future capital of the Russian Empire in the delta of the River Neva. On Hare Island the Emperor by tradition himself cut two pieces of green and, laying them in a cross, announced majestically: "Let the city stand here!"

Like a Titan he raised sleepy Russia to her feet. He achieved the impossible in only a few decades, creating a great world power. With untiring energy Peter set to building this northern outpost which would be "a window on Europe" for Russia, opening boundless naval horizons to the young state.

Thanks to gigantic efforts on the part of all Russia, the deserted banks of the Neva changed before their very eyes, gaining magnificent palaces, cathedrals and parks. St Petersburg is a masterpiece, the work of leading architects from all over the world, and is one of the most beautiful cities on the whole planet.

Grateful generations of descendants have carefully preserved the first house of the Northern Capital. Under the canopy of the park on the bank of the River Neva stands the small

wooden house in which Peter lived, just as it stood 300 years ago.

Go into the house. Everything is just as it was when its owner lived here. And it seems as though the bombadier of the Preobrazhensky Regiment, dressed in his ubiquitous master's uniform, drawing on his short pipe, has just stepped out for a moment...

Much has changed in the appearance of St Petersburg over the centuries. The carriages and droshkies which once adorned its streets are no longer to be seen, nor are the gaslights or the wooden cobbles. The whims of fashion have long forgot the luxurious dress of the ladies and their cavaliers, and the whole structure of city life has changed.

Dynamic and modern, today St Petersburg greets us with all

the noise of its multi-million inhabitants, the whirlpool of its streets, the glare of advertisements and a sea of lights. The tidal wave of people engulfs us carelessly and on its crest we see before us the unforgettable picture of endless lines of museums and palaces. It is impossible to picture St Petersburg in the evening without the footlights in the theatres, the ovations in the concert halls!

The old city is beautiful at any time of year. Succumbing to the ever-changing caprices of the northern climate, it is forever changing its dress, like an aged courtier aping the young, transforming its streets and embankments until they are unrecognisable. But there is something unchanging and eternal here, the spirit of the city, illuminated by the inspiration of many centuries of inhabitants.

The town of artists and composers, of thinkers and poets, of new scientific discoveries, St Petersburg has given the world all that is best in the human soul.

After many years of tragic suffering – wars, revolution, siege – the city has finally been given back its proud name, St Petersburg!

Rising like a phoenix from the ashes, the city has shaken off the dust of the past from its powerful wings. Now the rapid flight into the future has begun, and the city will shine like a bright star in the sky of worldwide fame as it stands on the threshold of its 300th anniversary.

*The Peter and
Paul Fortress on
Hare Island, Seen
From the Air*

17

*The Hermitage on Palace Embankment*

*The Strelka, Vasilyevsky Island*

*Nikolsky Cathedral*

*The Atlantes
by the Hermitage*

*The Birthday of St Petersburg*

*The Church of
the Resurrection
(The Saviour on
the Blood)*

*Religious Procession*

*Ioann, Metropolitan of St Petersburg and Ladoga*

*Alexei II, Patriarch of Moscow and All Russia*

*A Church Wedding*

53

*St Isaac's Cathedral*

*The Hermitage*

# White Nights

Weary of shining all day in the burning blue sky, from early dawn her magical rays opening up the buds and flowers and bringing out the young green leaves, towards evening the May sun sinks her golden head towards the night horizon.

Every day as she goes to sleep she paints the clouds and sky with the new, pure colours of the coming summer. But she sleeps for only a short time, covering the town with the dim twilight of the White Nights.

At this time the Empress Night comes into her own. Quietly she raises the many tonnes of the vast bridges over the Neva and graciously waves past the ships which are always hurrying off to far countries. Enslaved by her charm, thousands of people come out onto the embankments, singing and merry-making 'til morning!

Ghostly landscapes, the strumming of guitars, voices, the soft splash of water and the screeches of floating gulls all combine to form a single, unreal picture. The night damp falls over St Petersburg, warming itself by the water and granite walls which have basked in the sun all day. The freshness of the night and the warmth rising from the ground make the air elasitc and tangible. It envelopes us, the intoxicating aroma making our head spin and sending new life coursing through our veins.

The twilight hides people's faces as if at a masquerade. During the night hours your soul opens up, awakens to love. With the smell of lilac and water in the air, the city's silhouette seems like a mirage, covered with the silver coating of night beneath the transparent diamonds of the stars.

The Rostral Columns and the spire of the Admiralty seem to be drawn in charcoal against the night sky, and the gold of the dome of St Isaac's Cathedral dims.

In the quiet of night we can hear the ringing of the bells of the Cathedral of SS Peter and Paul. The sphinxes, thousands of years old, doze quietly, lulled by the soft lapping of the waves on the River Neva. Traffic lights blink on the empty Nevsky Prospekt and in the park on Arts Square Alexander Pushkin declaims his poetry just as he did hundreds of years ago.

At three o'clock exactly, the passage of ships ceases abruptly and the bridges drop down; the main avenues of the city, severed by the Neva, come to life once more for a short time. The middle of the night. Slowly the sickle moon fades. On one side of the city the horizon is still dark, but to the east the

sky is turning a rosy hue, reflected in numerous windows.
Night opens the bridges a second time! Their lights twinkling
as in some small toy box, the ships hurry to pass through the
eye of the needles that are the bridges before day comes.
They are sped on their way by the bared teeth of the lions
standing by the waters' edge.

With each minute dawn is drawing closer, and soon the sun
leaps on its red stallion into the sky, leaving behind a train of
fiery red. In a moment the night has gone, the sun taking over
rule of the skies, rising majestically above the roofs of St
Petersburg. Lifting his powerful hand, severe Neptune greets
the sun, and the statues mounting guard on the roof of the
Hermitage ceremoniously salute the omnipotent luminary...

The birds awake to greet the day and the ringing chimes of

the bells disturb the lovers sleeping on park benches. The trams test their voices, lorries rumble as they deliver deliciously smelling bread, and street sweepers begin swinging their eternal brooms on the empty streets.

The sun rises, presenting everyone with a new day. First she closes the night bridges, allowing the cars to pass along the streets, then she sends the lorries out to wash down the pavements with streams of cold water.

The sun polishes the spires of St Petersburg and the ship of the Admiralty to a blinding sparkle, greeting the angel above the fortress, and then returns to earth, casting her golden drops of sun onto the windows of the city, saying to us all as she wakes us: "Good morning!"

# The Venice of the North

*You* can wander through the streets, squares and parks of St Petersburg and find something new every time. Jump onto a motorboat and you will see another of the wonders of the world – the Venice of the North. To see the whole of St Petersburg with its 42 islands from the water, you have to travel over 1,000 km along 49 rivers and 19 canals.

So, off we go! Eyes blinded by the sun, seaspray splashing across our faces, a warm summer breeze running through our hair.

The Summer Gardens recedes across the stern, a branch of luxuriant foliage hanging down to the water surface as if to take a dip. The vast outline of the Mikhail Fortress glides by and we catch a glimpse of bustling Sadovaya Street; looking up to the clouds we see the sun glinting off the cupolas and twisted blue and white domes of the Church of the Resurrection. For a moment we take in once more all the marvel of its mosaics. The elegant lampposts on the Italian Bridge nod in greeting as we pass.

High up, spires and towers swim through the blue of the sky, while down below majestic Classical palaces vie eternally with the ornamental levity of the Baroque and Renaissance.

We move into deep gloom as we pass beneath the bridge that carries Nevsky Prospekt, and suddenly we see the immense crags of the colonnade of the Kazan Cathedral hanging over us. Before we have had time to take in the grandeur of this part of Nevsky our eyes are dragged forward once more to peer at the tiny detail on the golden-winged gryphons who support the openwork Bank Bridge. Here, on the banks of Admiralty, Kazan and Saviour islands, we find the most intimate corners of the Northern Venice.

The tall embankments hang over us like the steep sides of a canyon. The permanent calm of the softly rippling surface of the water reflects the ever-changing multi-coloured facades along the water's edge. The sun passes playfully over the

water and the numerous ducks and seagulls who disturb its mirror surface.

The widest of all the 588 bridges in St Petersburg is the Blue Bridge. As we approach it we see the golden dome of St Isaac's Cathedral glinting and then the bright light of the sunny day is replaced by the thick darkness of an icy cold tunnel. A small dot of light in the distance marks the exit, but we shall be shivering slightly by the time we have passed through the 99 metres of the belly of the bridge.

The watery elements to this day cannot make their peace with the granite embankments. Each year the city experiences several small floods, the swelling Neva raising the waters in the rivers and canals almost to the level of the pavement, covering the lower parts of the town. Statistics show that once every hundred years the sea engulfs the streets and squares of St Petersburg like the legendary Atlantis.

Here, by the Blue Bridge, is a memorial to mark the catastrophic floods of the past. Fortunately, St Petersburg, built by the city fathers to stand for centuries, always emerges the victor in this battle with the waters, marked by Neptune's broken trident mounted upon an obelisk.

Beyond very twist and turn in the canals and rivers lie new revelations. We could admire for hours on end the Nikolsky Cathedral with its bell tower seeming to rise out of the water itself, and New Holland, currently enjoying a renaissance.

Let us hurry on to the wide open spaces of the Neva! It is her majestic character which determined the building of St Petersburg and her embankments are adorned with a necklace of superb palaces and parks. The Strelka or spit of Vasilyevsky Island projects into the Neva like the prow of some ancient ship lying at anchor, cutting it into two streams. Once this expanse was filled with the masts of the ships

which came to the Northern Venice from all ends of the earth. Today, as 150 years ago, a canon shot fired from the bastion of the Peter and Paul Fortress marks midday, raising flocks of seagulls for many miles around.

Bridges run from bank to bank like wings, linking the embankments on which stand the Hermitage and the Fortress, the Admiralty and the University, St Isaac's Cathedral and the Academy of Arts. The whole planet knows this magnificent, stately, Nevsky facade of St Petersburg.

Always a special day in the life of the city on the Neva is the birthday of St Petersburg, and after the numerous celebrations during this day in May the sky above the Neva is lit up with sprays of fireworks. And old Petersburg, not without its weaknesses, like us all, but an aristocrat and a gentleman, shakes off the dust of many years and receives our congratulations with all the charm of youth: "Happy birthday, O city of Peter, the Venice of the North!"

# *A* Walk in the Summer Gardens

*The* Summer Gardens have their own particular beauty at any time of the year. In the summer you will find much-needed cool and quiet in its shady avenues, time to rest from the hustle and bustle of a large city.

During an Indian summer the tops of the trees are crowned with golden patterns, penetrated by the warms rays of the autumn sun. The whole park is covered with a soft carpet formed of the leaves which fall to our feet like stars from the sky.

On such days it is pleasant to walk, our footsteps rustling through the autumn gold, drinking in the smell of departing summer.

I am sure I will not be mistaken if I say that this is the favourite time for the city's inhabitants to walk in the Summer

Gardens, which they affectionately call just "Letny" or "Summer".

After the long, hard northern winter, spring is always a holiday in St Petersburg, celebrated anew each year in the gardens with blinding fireworks of young, green leaves. At last the wooden boxes which hide the marble statues from the cold for many months are taken away, and we see the garden youthful and fresh once more, just as we remember it on our first visit long ago in the days of our childhood. Only the tall, broad trees reveal the reverent age of the Summer Gardens.

Peter the Great probably saw the Summer Gardens anew each time just as we do. "His Imperial Majesty himself drew up" the plan for the park and in the spring of 1704 the park was laid out "better than at the French King's Versailles". With his

natural energy and enthusiasm, Peter set about building up his beloved gardens.

In those far off days there were numerous fountains with golden fish, streams of water flashed in the sunlight, the trees were trimmed into all sorts of animal shapes. The air was filled with the singing of many birds, skilfully hidden in cages among the thick foliage, a hedge ran along the avenue forming green walls with niches for the statues.

The gardens clearly took their name from that of the Summer Palace, a work "in the Dutch style" by Domenico Trezzini, known simply as Andrei Ivanovich in Russia.

As old as the city itself, the gardens were to be the site of celebrations and assemblies and the reception of foreign envoys. At the magnificent balls in the imperial residence all

the guests were served with wine and even the women were not left out when it came to drinking ... vodka!

During such receptions the gardens were always locked shut so that no one could dare to refuse to drink "to the health of the colonel" – Peter the Great. Such feasts were always completed by "fire amusements", excellent fireworks accompanied by the trumpeting voices of the elephants which lived across on the other side of the Fontanka.

To this day portly Krylov, surrounded by the heroes of his fables, sits deep in thought beneath a canopy of maples.

In the Tea and Coffee Houses we can always see marvellous exhibitions of the works of St Petersburg's painters, sculptors and applied artists.

White swans glide across the surface of the Karpiev Pond as

they did hundreds of years ago. In the shady avenues the white marble antique statues, brought here centuries ago from sunny Italy, stand proudly on their pedestals. The Emperor loved these statues and showed them off to all his foreign guests.

The great age of the Summer Gardens seems to give them an atmosphere of calm and wisdom. We have only to step across the threshold and they meet us like an old friend, shaking the tops of their heavy trees in greeting.

When we leave, they sadden slightly and will stand, lonely, beneath the deep snows of endless winter, living in expectation of the next, long-awaited meeting.

*Pushkin*

108

*Petrodvorets*

*Pavlovsk*

# Christmas Eve

*Winter* lasts a long time in St Peterburg. Tired of waiting, the night sky lights up at last with billions of sparkling snowflakes. Falling, falling slowly, they cover the whole city with a white carpet.

Waking up in the morning, we greet with joy the magical mystery of nature. During the night the frost has covered all the windows with pearly patterns, leaving carefully plumped up fat cushions of snow on the roof and windowsills and an even blanket of snow on the roads.

Driving away the rainy days of late autumn, the long-awaited sun makes its appearance in the sky, pouring its winter rays over the city. Reflected in every snowflake, the sun lights up millions of sparks in the air as we pass. The snow

beneath our feet crunches as we take hearty gulps of icy winter air.

The trees in the parks are covered with hoar-frost, like the finest coral. The red-breasted bull-finch leaps from branch to branch in a business-like manner, while the eternal urban sparrows wallow merrily in the first downy snow. Happy children, glad that winter has arrived at last, noisily build snowmen with red carrots for noses and old buckets on their heads. A whole gang of red-cheeked children slide down icy hills with joyful squeals.

What can compare with the beauty of the Russian winter? Old women slide down hills with their granchildren, recalling their own childhood. Fathers build snow fortresses for their sons

and then help storm them, completely forgetting the respectability of their age.

Old men sit on benches reading a paper, softly rocking prams. The babies in the prams are warmly wrapped up in thick layers of blankets against the winter frost, only their noses peeping out! Forgetting all about supper and their mothers' admonitions in the heat of their games, boys cut to and fro across the ice on their skates until dark, when the first street lights begin to shine.

At this hour it is good to amble unhurriedly through the wintry parks and then relax in the warm of your home or set off for the theatre! By the theatre door there is a festive bustle, while inside the boxes are lit, the orchestra is tuning up... and

at last the lights go down. Obeying the magic wand waved by the conductor, the curtain shoots up and the music and magical dancing take us away into the fairytale world of ballet.

With a light wave of the hand from the maestro, we are whirled away in a second to another century, to another town in another country. The waves of music roll over us and lull us into a dream and we can no longer tell where we are: are we imagining this or is it real? With imperceptible movements of his fingers, the conductor magics a ballerina up on the stage. The scenery changes, and under the heat of the footlights, Good, which always emerges triumphant, does battle with Evil, and the omnipotent and shrewd maestro

raises a tidal wave of feelings in our hearts. Oh, the theatre is a magician, a crystal castle where dreams become reality and Cinderella becomes a princess, if only for a few hours!

On Christmas Eve, the snow-laden city is illuminated by the multi-coloured lights of Christmas trees in the windows of buildings. The sickle moon hangs in the black sky amid a myriad of stars, giving out its flickering light over the city. The frost scatters its silver, which catches on the eyelashes of the girl on your arm. Miracles truly happen at this time of year, and perhaps you will find yourself at a New Year's ball in St Petersburg! Forgotten traditions are now being revived in this great city, filling our hearts with warmth and the expectation of happiness, and maybe you will find that happiness here.

*The Admire*

*University Embankment*

*The Winter Canal*

*The Golden
Dome of
St Isaac's
Cathedral*

*The Sphinxes from Ancient Thebes*

*The Bronze Horseman — Monument to Peter the Great*

*The Smolny and Nikolsky Cathedrals*

*Ice on the
River Neva*

133

*St Petersburg has not only walruses but also polar bears – in the zoo!*

*Fishing in Winter on the Neva and the Gulf of Finland*

Bank Bridge

*The Kirov
Ballet*

St Petersburg
Jazz Club

*The Music-Hall*

*New Year's Ball
in St Petersburg*

151

*Palace Square*

153